5 REASONS MEN LOSE EMOTIONAL INTIMACY.

BY

Dr TIMOTHY KESSINGTON

approval from the publisher or creator.

TABLE OF CONTENTS

TABLE OF CONTENT

ABOUT THE AUTHOR

Dr. TIMOTHY KESSINGTON is a licensed psychologist in the state of texas. he is a certified counselor on marriage and relationship/mental health. He is passionate to the core to see people in relationships happy and couples achieve the best out of every relationship.

Introduction:

All is good until all of a sudden there is no longer a fire. There was a moment when the energy that coursed through your veins would merely make you two stare at one another. Regarding everything, you were in accord. Your chemistry lit up the room whenever you were among other people. All day, you had each other on your mind. Now, however, you continue to check your phone and it is not ringing as often. What took place?

CHAPTER 1. No physical attraction.

As our lifestyles change, so do our bodies. You could have put on a few pounds if your lifestyle has become sedentary. While some spouses consider it to be insignificant, others believe it to be a deal-breaker. Talk over it with your spouse without becoming defensive.

"When we first met, what did you discover that was so beautiful about me—my figure or my intelligence?" a woman asked her husband. "I noticed you walking across the beach," the husband retorted. You looked good. I fell in love with your intelligence after getting to know you. Your intellect was not visible to me at the beach. It's probably reasonable to argue that maintaining emotional connection requires at least a modicum of physical attractiveness. It is an essential feeling for all people.

Chapter 2: Lack of spontaneity.

An important factor in relationships is acceptance. Livflexiblyible permits you to make mistakes together and convert them into impromptu, uplifting, and delightful occasions. For instance, rather than whining about how horrible a room looks, try helping your spouse

decorate it better.
Participate by painting,
adding more mess, using
vibrant colors, and then
dousing each other with
paint. This impromptu
humor communicates to
your spouse that it's not a
big issue. Even if there
could be some cleanup
later, two people can
accomplish it more quickly
than one. Play with each

other. Things may become lively when one is impulsive. Your partner has to have leeway to make errors in your relationship. It is necessary to allow for errors to be made by both sides. Emotional connection in a marriage is lost when there is no room for flexibility or impromptu activities.

CHAPTER 3. Extended periods of tension.

In reaction to stress, the human body produces the hormone cortisol. Depression and ultimately mental disorders are caused by ongoing stress. Stress wears individuals out and makes them irritable. It is impossible to have emotional closeness while sad. The good news is that you can control your stress. Determine the source of the stress in your life and address it head-on. If it's a sequence of incidents, read, practice meditation, get more exercise, and enjoy some nice music. Engage in activities that help you unwind. Sexual intimacy may be lost as a result of ongoing stress. Make careful not to overindulge in drugs that impair cognition, such as alcohol. They could result in health issues rather than close emotional relationships.

CHAPTER 4. Health issues.

Everybody sometimes has bad days, but when serious health issues like diabetes, lupus, cancer, heart disease, or high blood pressure are present, symptoms may become worse. Your marriage may suffer as a result of the stress. Anybody may feel the effects of potential operations, scheduling regular doctor's visits, taking prescription drugs as directed, and keeping an eye on their health. Noticing your spouse's effort in these occurrences is tough. The good news is that a lot of individuals manage their partner's disease and go on to have happy marriages. Under these circumstances, it is recommended that professional assistance be sought because untreated health issues may lead to a loss of emotional closeness.

CHAPTER 5: Conflicts.

The establishment of marriage is undermined by far too many conflicts and battles. Find a way to "let it go." There may be occasions when a pair can't agree on anything. Just accept your discrepancies and proceed on to the following item. Since you are married and share a life, there will always be

something else to do.
During heated arguments,
people sometimes say
things they later regret.
Arguments like this lead to
a lack of emotional
closeness.

CONCLUSION.

It's reasonable to conclude that guys don't experience much emotional closeness. Lack of chemistry, inability to have fun on the spur of the moment, long-term stress, health issues, and an excessive number of arguments and setbacks may all ruin a marriage. It is possible to fix all of these things and make the relationship emotionally fulfilling again. Numerous certified experts are available to help with these kinds of problems and provide a long-term solution for you.

www.ingramcontent.com/pod-product-compliance
Lightning Source LLC
Chambersburg PA
CBHW050758250726
48662CB00005B/2297